Azaria Poems

Chantelle Lowe

Azaria Poems

Chantelle Lowe

All rights reserved. No part of this book may be reproduced or transmitted in any form or by any means, electronic or mechanical, including photocopying, recording, or by any information storage and retrieval system, without permission in writing from the publisher.

Published by Chantelle Griffin, originally known as Chantelle Lowe, in 2020

Interior layout by Chantelle Lowe

Cover by Chantelle Lowe

Photograph: Chantelle and Uluru at sunset
Lowe family trip to Uluru, 17 August 1980

Catalogue-in-Publication details available
from the National Library of Australia

paperback ISBN: 978-0-6487305-8-3

Also available in hardback
ISBN: 978-0-6487305-9-0

Copyright © Chantelle Griffin, originally known as Chantelle Lowe, 2020

Dedication

In loving memory of the beautiful baby
I met at Uluru on 17 August 1980.

Contents

Azaria Poems

A baby	1
A dream	2
A lie to a young child	5
A love so strong	10
A soul	12
A story	14
A whisper and you were there	16
Azaria	17
Barry Boettcher	18
Celebration of life	19
Convenience	20
Disbelief	21

Do you know who I am?	22
Forgiveness	23
Group	24
Her spirit	27
I remember	28
In a moment	29
In memory of Azaria	30
Instilled in memory	32
Into eternity	33
John Bryson	34
Justice	35
Justice in jeopardy	36
Justice Michael Kirby	38
Let those grieve	39
Lindy	42
Looking back on my past	44
Melbourne	46
Memories I have lost	47
My past	49
Neville Dawson	50
Opera (Lindy)	51
People suffer	52
Played as pawns	53
Power	54

Remembering Azaria	57
Sally	58
Sense	61
Serenity (my mother)	62
Staying at places	64
Time ceases	65
Time on this world	67
The Witness (my mother)	68
This is the path I walk on	70
Waiting	72
Where to turn	73
Whispering	74
Undeciding factor	75
Your name	76

Photographs

Slides of the Lowe family trip to Uluru, 17 August 1980

1. Uluru from the ranger's office	4
2. Climb up Uluru	11
3. Climb up Uluru	15
4. Climb up Uluru	26
5. Climb up Uluru	31
6. Chantelle and unknown lady on Uluru	37
7. Climb down Uluru	48
8. Uluru in the afternoon	56
9. Chantelle and Ululru at sunset	60
10. Uluru at sunset	66

Acknowledgements

I would like to thank Greg Lowe, Sally Shaw, Michael Chamberlain (deceased), Lindy Chamberlain-Creighton, Rick Creighton, Judy West (deceased), Wally and Margot Goodwin, Stuart Tipple, John Bryson, Barry Boettcher, Neville Dawson and so many more who showed courage and support.

More recently, I would like to thank John Buck, as well as the Northern Territory for providing access to the archive material.

Foreward

On 17 August 1980, my parents drove from Alice Springs to Uluru with me in a four-wheel drive vehicle. I was a tiny seventeen month old, due to be placed in a tent at the same campsite as the Chamberlains half an hour later. Greg lost sight of Lindy for a brief moment near the tent, Sally lost sight of Lindy for 6-10 minutes.

In the words of Greg Lowe, 'It could have been us.'

Chantelle Lowe

A baby

A baby, a small child,
a memory inside.
I see her, so fragile,
yet happy and smiling.
A small baby, that died.
For such a short time,
she affected so many.
She is remembered,
and she is loved.

Chantelle Lowe

A dream

Remember my name when I am done,
remember my name for I am not one.
Remember the child that loved and cried,
remember the child that slept and died.
A dream could not have ever foreseen,
a dream could not explain what had been.
A dream was the thought of the prosecutors,
a dream which seeped through to the onlookers.
Colouring the objects held by the innocent,
colouring the minds of the indecent.
Colouring the numerous pages of writing,
colouring the path of those left fighting.
An image that held on deeper than blood,
an image that cast doubt in a tidal flood.
An image more potent than any stain,
an image covering those who remain.
Details fabricated or to be left unsaid,

Chantelle Lowe

details painting over the truth unread.
Details showing through immorality,
details bringing home and setting free.

Chantelle Lowe

Photograph 1: Uluru from the ranger's office, 17 August 1980.

A lie to a young child

I am the truth behind the lie,
do not think that I do not know;
that I do not know what you did.
What you did was unspeakable,
it crossed all boundaries,
it defiled all natures of justice,
it crippled my mother.
Do not think that I do not know what you did,
destroying the tests,
losing the evidence.
Whispering in my mother's ear to make her snigger,
keeping my father away.
Do not think that you can lie to me,
When an eight an half month pregnant woman
was kept on a wooden stool for five to six hours
and vomited.
Do not think you can cover up the photos

of the clothing picked up and laid incorrectly.
Did you think you could lie to me?
When my father fell apart.
Did you think you could make a false story fact?
When I saw my mother's tears fall from
her face and into my lap.
Did you think you could cover up the effort
made to break my mother?
Putting her in a room with no air-conditioning
with a sick baby and giving her no help.
Denying childcare for her children.
Who were you lying to?
When you destroyed my mother's faith in you.
You were lying to me because I was there.
I waited for my mother at court,
I waited with Judy West.
I ran because I was alive,
I was a little girl,
and I saw what you did to my mother.
I was the one that hugged her,
I was the one that loved her,
I was the one who gave her support.
I could not heal her wounds,
they were too deep.

Chantelle Lowe

They were made by people who knew
what they were doing,
they were made by you.
My mother saw Azaria's feet kicking
the blanket loose in Lindy's arms.
My father saw Lindy return from the tent empty handed.
My mother heard Azaria's cry,
a cry that was cut short.
The dingo was tracked,
and you lied.
Les Harris the dingo expert knew,
and you lied.
When you slept at night,
my mother cried.
When you had done the deed,
you left my mother to bring justice.
All those judges and it was left to a young mother.
She was in my arms,
and she cried.
She loved me and she cried.
I want you to know,
I know you lied.
I care not why when all I need is to know,
I know it was done

Chantelle Lowe

to break my mother.
When you went home to sleep,
I was there,
in my arms she cried.
After everything that was done,
I cannot mend what you did,
the wound is too deep.
You denied me knowing my mother as she was.
What did you think when you left a young child
to support the main witness?
What were you thinking when you forced that onto me?
Am I that dispensable to you?
Did you think I would not notice?
Did you think I would forget?
I did not ask you to nominate me as my mother's support.
I did not ask you to do what you did.
You do not have any right to leave me to pick up the pieces.
You do not have any right to get me to mend your mistakes.
I refuse to part of your lies,
I just wanted my mother to have support.
I was a child,
you lied to me,
and expected me to comfort the crown witness.
You lied to me

when you tried to break my mother.
You lied when you left her without a care.
You lied when you left her behind.
You betrayed her
when you forced me to clean up your mess.
Remember me in your old age,
remember that I was there,
remember that you could have been better,
remember that when all is done,
I remember too.

Chantelle Lowe

Photograph 2: climb up Uluru, 17 August 1980.

A love so strong

To me this day is very special,
one of much regret.
When everybody thought,
what nature could not guess.
When everybody knew,
but no one wanted to believe.
That a beautiful little girl,
had been taken from a loving mother's arms.
On a night when no one
could have believed
of a love for a young girl, so strong.
A love so strong,
it faced the lies,
and held a wonderful
lady together,
in times of hardship.

Chantelle Lowe

A soul

A name I know, a face I saw, a time away,
and yet I remember.
It calls to me, it remembers me, it knows I was there.
How can I forget, it wasn't up to me.
They knew, and it wasn't up to me.
They knew and they went on.
Corruption destroyed their core,
and they went on.
All the while it was not up to me,
and they assumed it was up to them.
Corruption seeped into their arteries and guided their judgement.
How was I to know, and how was I to forget?
All along this is what had been,
and all along I knew what it was.
I lived knowing the past, remembering its judgement.
How can I forget when what was done was beyond belief,
and in all this one thing was lost.

Chantelle Lowe

It was small and fragile, it smiled, and everyone had smiled with it.
A soul.

Chantelle Lowe

Photograph 3: climb up Uluru, 17 August 1980.

A story

Antipathy to succeed.
A story within a story of a light so grey,
an area so wrong,
and all the time I knew.
It was painful and I knew.
A way around the world, a glimpse,
and the confusion was immense.
Places I have been to and people I have met,
A rarity on this small earth,
and I am amidst it all.
A time, a memory, and I am there.
All it was, all it had to be,
and I did not know.
A creation, so ugly yet real,
the savagery of humankind,
the callous face which raises its head.
I saw it, and I remember it.

Chantelle Lowe

A whisper and you were there

Along time ago, a child that died.
Here I hold in my heart the memory of a little girl.
The tester of faith, the power of freedom,
facing lies and falsehood.
The testimony of the innocent calling out to be heard,
and you heard, from where ever you were.
A mother that grieved, a family that remembered.
It tore against the memory like the pain of solid ice crashing into the skin.
It called you, and you saw.
You rested your hand on those who were there,
You pushed them forward and kept them true.
Even when all was crashing down,
and hope seemed far away.
There was a whisper, and you were there.
Holding on so tight to those you loved,
and those who loved you.

Azaria

I will never forget her.
Though I do not remember her,
in person.
I imagine her,
a sweet eyed child
with happiness forever trapped
in her soul
given to her by those who love her.

Barry Boettcher

You stand,
and you know your research better than this courtroom.
You understand the results better than what is happening,
and you never gave up.
You knew what had to be done,
and you went beyond what was asked of you.
Even when some thought it was too late,
you continued relentlessly.
Your passion and your determination created ripples,
which could be seen by others.
You held out hope,
seeking truthful answers.
A dedication defying the magnitude of the situation.

Celebration of life

There are people I know not where,
in this way I find my own.
The little gathering that happens here,
in a setting far from home.
Nothing could compel me away,
from the event in which I take part.
On a fine and memorable day,
holding memories close to my heart.
People start to wander in,
shaking hands and saying names.
Remembering a time from within,
relaxing now in silent frames.
As all those have come to gather,
sit under the shade and remember.

Convenience

It is inexplicably clean,
yet tainted in every way.
Its violence consumes.
As others may show dismay,
as it shows pity.
To cower at it,
to be awestruck.
Would be malevolent to its nature.
But to compose, and resist,
is nature within itself.
And this forms the convenience to us.
A shallow grimness, to be pulled forward,
with no speculation.
But to erase is to forget,
and forgotten, it would come again.
To form a new way in the old,
and crumple the edges in itself.

Disbelief

A time in a place long forgotten.
Where I was, where it happened.
I know it was a hard journey,
It took so many, so long.
All this time I remember,
I remember because I was there.
It upsets me that all this could happen,
so little was known,
so much believed.
Through all this I saw it happen,
and I did not want to believe
that it could.

Chantelle Lowe

Do you know who I am?

Who am I?
Do you know who I am?
Who am I?
Do you know who I am?
In the scheme of things,
where do I fit in?

Chantelle Lowe

Forgiveness

It is time to forgive those who didn't know,
it is time to forgive those who did wrong.
It is time to thank those who helped
prove a dingo did it, and move on.

Chantelle Lowe

Group

A group,
a group gathered in support.
They link hands, and they are stronger.
A heartfelt plea,
accusations.
A wolf, unknown to humankind.
A carrier of distortion,
and that is enough.
Take it, manipulate it because it does not concern you,
but in a way it does.
Hiding negligence, lack of warning.
Hiding the real knowledge.
Painting a picture that covers up.
Integrity is flung from the tallest height and smashes on the ground below.
Truth replaced by madness for the sake of the unbelievers.
Tumbling to the ground comes the whole picture painted white,
and in the areas of grey comes forth the truth.

Chantelle Lowe

A solicited manifestation of the mind crumbles,
in a glimmer of hope.
Standing strong are the witnesses, standing strong is the support,
and over all this flies a small fragment called truth,
covered in the piles of knowledge,
beyond the investigation.
It flies above the courtroom and it sees,
this is not the end, nor is it the beginning.
Corruption runs deep in here,
but support is stronger.
People giving up their time, and their own finances,
to present the truth.
Experts, never giving up their cause.
When behind all this,
the bombardment of lies which led people to disbelieve the truth.
The carefully left out pieces of information,
and the carefully covered up.
A shame which crossed the faces of the deceived,
to have to call the truth a lie.

Chantelle Lowe

Photograph 4: climb up Uluru, 17 August 1980.

Her spirit

Even in the life I have,
I remember her still.
Azaria's spirit is with us,
and has been every step of the way.
Driving us forward,
watching us as we get on with our lives.
Remembering the past.

Chantelle Lowe

I remember

Today I remember how fortunate I am to be alive,
Today I remember I was saved and another child died.
Azaria Chamberlain may you rest in God's hands.

In a moment

How powerful a moment is,
have you ever wondered?

In a moment, your baby is gone.
In a moment, you are found guilty.
In a moment, a tiny little jacket is found.

In a moment, you stand at the Sydney Town Hall,
and you speak from the heart,
and you speak because you know
so much is depending on you.

In a moment, you remember
running in the waiting room
for the witnesses,
and you are waiting for your parents.

Chantelle Lowe

Photograph 5: climb up Uluru, 17 August 1980.

In memory of Azaria

May a spirit so small go in peace,
it washes over my soul,
and I feel it within.
It graced the world,
and created memories so deep,
in a world that was not ready to accept.
All the while this little spirit loved and lived,
and was loved.
It touched people's hearts,
and broke them.
For it only touched the earth a little while,
whispering in the corner of times eye.
It had all anything could want,
then left so quickly,
leaving those who loved behind.

Chantelle Lowe

Instilled in memory

Symmetrical apparitions brazen my mind,
as though I were someone else.
And all this time I wonder,
if it was meant to be.
Nothing truly understood,
until too late.
Giving satirical form to harsh reality.
It opened my mind,
a very hard fight.
I knew about it,
while others forgot.
The physical scarring,
lay blatant on the reaches of my mind.
Was I supposed to know,
did someone deem it of me?
A terrible disgrace,
one which I have instilled in memory.

Into eternity

Smile in the way I remember,
smile in the love that was found.
Transforming a young life into eternity,
remembering the short time that has been.

Chantelle Lowe

John Bryson

An intelligence so humbled by wisdom,
looking on without bias,
knowing that this is important.
All the while events take place,
anything can be written and is,
in this time truth is left far behind.
Trapped in this world it meets someone,
this person knows the language of the courtroom,
this person can see.
His eyes are open, and he writes like no other.
He writes the events as they are,
in this way truth has picked him out,
and allowed him to be heard.

Justice

Killing takes strangeness out of reality,
what would we be without lies,
covering the pattern of what we see,
until the common truth dies.

This reality which we seek so much,
turns anonymity on its head.
While things are not so human to touch,
when all we hear is what is said.

And while strangers reel in dismay,
at what is being taken over,
in the world of humans in this way,
to hold up, then take and cover.

In a world where what is portrayed,
is taken, used, and then betrayed.

Chantelle Lowe

Photograph 6: Chantelle and unknown lady on Uluru, 17 August 1980.

Justice in jeopardy

Justice in jeopardy,
and we all hold hands.
Justice in jeopardy,
and people are brought together,
from all walks of life.
An innocent lady,
a cost so deep.
A knowledge so strong,
it burns into the minds of many,
and calls them forward.

Chantelle Lowe

Justice Michael Kirby

A letter,
was all it was.
If you think injustices have been done,
do not give up.
A letter, and it gave support,
it gave strength,
in a time so dark, it became hope.
A letter of sincerity,
heartfelt and dignified.

Chantelle Lowe

Let those grieve

Discouragement destroys everything,
and disappointment comes with it.
Killing time with eternity.
Does it really mean it?
In this hideous world of lies,
which is damnation
onto the face of creation,
killing time and essence.
What did you say?
What did I see?
When everyone left,
were you there?
Killing everything, or so it seemed,
but what does the world read into this?
When everything is gone
and all that is left is you and me.
Will you carry on to be,

Chantelle Lowe

the asphyxiation?
Placing the hand over what is.
But is this yours?
Do you really mean it?
Taking away life is difficult at the best of times,
but to take life,
then torture those who surround it,
this is vicious,
very vile.
What creature made you?
Obviously not one with humanity.
Killing the soul,
but wait, you did not have one.
Torturers do not feel love,
they live in a careless world.
Is that what made you?
To not let those grieve,
those who truly cared.
Did you dare, to lend out a hand,
or did you abuse it?
Like you abused those with truth in their hearts.
Those with the power to love,
those with the power to heal.
Those who know,

and loved,
and came through.
Those who shone,
before the powers that be.

Chantelle Lowe

Glimmer of hope and essence of air,
beating down on beautiful dark hair.
Laughter swept through with a proud mother's smile,
with life so precious it lasted but a while.

Hope held in faith and a loving husband's hand,
bring joy of innocence and naivety for the land.
Sadness caressed the child in a loving mother's arm,
when a gut-wrenching cry called out all to alarm.

No matter which way the elegant lady turned;
judgement, fear and the wail of rumour burned.
So intense was the faith it held God in sight,
when mistruths and innuendo darkened the light.

Fear not fair lady who cherished your child,
losing her in the worst manner out in the wild.

Chantelle Lowe

For truth has a way of seeking us out,
Dismissing the rumours among so much doubt.

In time held strong with those who believe,
the loss of a beautiful baby and the silence to grieve.

Looking back at my past

Look back and I see my past,
Looking forword and I see my future.
I cry and I know,
what it is that I am crying for.
Twenty-three years to this day,
Azaria died.
I am twenty-four and alive.
My mother remembers
but prefers not to.
I remember and I wonder why.
Did all this suffering come to nought?
I dry my tears and the sky rains,
crying on my window.
Again I hold my mother up,
as she hides from remembering.
A new script on the horizon,
a new beginning to an end.

Chantelle Lowe

What happened in the aftermath,
I keep asking myself that.
We lost relatives and friends,
who turned away.
I lost my chance to make friends at all.
A small child with the precious gift of life,
and I am still mourning.

Chantelle Lowe

Melbourne

When end comes to end,
I must leave and go back.
My journey's been fine,
I'll never forget that.
The place I wish to be will always be home.
For there I shall remember those glorious moments,
which I treasured up here in Melbourne.
That I hope shall never be forgotten.

Chantelle Lowe

Memories I have lost

Memories I have, lost and jumbled,
yet they stay there,
and parts I remember.
I know I am different.
One foot in one world,
one foot in the other.
Somehow I have to journey back,
to find out who I am.
Somewhere along the line,
I lost who I was.
I was protected from it,
or it was deliberately left out.
Now I have to go back,
to discover who I am.

Chantelle Lowe

Photograph 7: climb down Uluru, 17 August 1980.

My past

My past, my history.
My place in time.
Where I am in the scheme of things.
To be me and no other.
This is my past,
this is who I am.

Chantelle Lowe

Neville Dawson

A picture truly paints more words than can be expressed,
and brought across in such a lasting way.
A determination heartfelt,
which covers the impressions transfixed in time.
A journey which has led the creator to a depth of understanding,
a shared experience.
Knowledge unravelled slowly, like the petals unfolding to the sun.
Sincerity touched by kindness.
A hand with the skill to transform words, expression and thought.
Painstakingly simple, yet so strong.
Caressed by small drops of sweat revealing dedication,
and a masterpiece is born.

Opera (Lindy)

Floating down the stairs into a world of disbelief.
Eternity on its shoulders, heaving forward,
this is reality.
A night so dazzling it conquers all,
bestilled by the excitement and nervousness.
Take with it what you will.
Anticipation.
One night, a time away,
seeing, believing.
Embracing the moment,
Tranquillised in raw emotion.
Capturing the essence,
a rare moment,
which embraces gratitude.

People suffer

The price which courses through my veins,
of what was known and what was done.
It is a price I live with,
in the back of my mind.
Of what has taken place in the past,
this obscene monstrosity created by the human mind.
Exaggerated to benefit other people's wants,
but in the end people suffer.
My family suffered at the hands of people's beliefs,
because some people only hear what they want to.

Played as pawns

Guilty are those who speak,
Guilty are those who say another.
Guilty are those who preach in light of day,
then send people off into the dim dark night.
Guilty are they of trespass,
Guilty are they of perjury.
The sins of immorality creep up their soul.
Guilty are those who stay and fight,
for the preachers of the dawn.
For nothing is as what it seems,
when people are played as pawns.

Power

All the while I know, and knowing is enough,
of what happened, and what my parents went through.
I remember them going to court for the trial,
I remember waiting for them to return.
I know what went on, and this is when I remember.
I remember all the wrong that was done,
all the harm that others did.
I remember and that is enough.
I remember travelling when my mother went and spoke at the rallies.
Deep down I remember.
It was hard, but the fight was even harder.
To go against a justice system which convicted a woman of total innocence.
The truth was covered up by a fabricated story with misleading evidence.
How can I forget the incompetence shown by the justice system,
which took so long to redeem.

Chantelle Lowe

Once the corruption began it was so easy to cling on to.
The principles of madness creating a blanket of wrong doing.
The morals of upholding corruption had been easier for those in power.
Covering over the negligence and wrong doing as though it were right,
created holes which came to unravel the fabric of power.
Power used in corruption to feed tales to the masses,
it came undone.

Chantelle Lowe

Photograph 8: Uluru in the afternoon, 17 August 1980.

Remembering Azaria

A girl,
a child.
Loving, knowing, laughing.
A celebration of life,
two months old,
knowing happiness.
This is the way she is remembered.
A happy youngster,
loving every moment of life.
Loved by those left behind.

Sally

Everything anyone could have hoped she would be,
A person with strength which carried her on.
There are not many who could have stood up against so much,
who could have made such a difference.
An ordinary, down to earth, no nonsense woman,
who stood up because it was the right thing to do.
A farm girl who did not mess around when there was hard work to be done,
with parents who had taught her to do what was right.
She did what she believed anyone else would have done,
in her position, with her knowledge.
She had grown up with the expectation that the justice system would be fair to people.
When it failed,
she took it upon herself to make sure that it was done.
A hard working girl, who grew up on farm,
the youngest daughter,

Chantelle Lowe

a young wife and mother,
who did what she had to do.

Chantelle Lowe

Photograph 9: Chantelle and Uluru at sunset, 17 August 1980.

Sense

I have an immense feeling inside,
it has come from the past.
Tracing its roots to a moment in time.
A young life died.
No reason given,
no answer why.
And in all this,
I was by my mother's side.
How fortunate am I,
in this moment?
Yet I carry immense pain,
from a moment which changed everything,
and the world as I knew it
died.
Inside I could feel my soul cry,
it was filled with rage,
and loss.

Serenity (my mother)

So serene is she, the guiding light travelling in the darkness.
I wanted to be with her, I wanted to hold her hand.
She possessed strength which was beyond me,
it was greater than many could ever encounter.
I wanted to comfort her, let her know that everything would be all right,
but I couldn't, and neither could anyone else.
She was born with a natural beauty so deep it enveloped her soul,
the inner strength guided her on against persecution.
She rose, like a single white flame fluttering above the torture,
knowing not to look down, not to give up, not to give in.
She believed in something so pure, so rare to behold,
it was truth, and she bore it with pride above the accusations.
Above the wrong doing, above all the lies.
It held her together, as no one else could,
and I wanted to be there, I wanted to comfort her,
when no one was there to protect her.
She held on for the sake of her beliefs, she held on for the sake of justice,

Chantelle Lowe

she held on for the sake of those who were wrongly accused.
She was the pure essence of truth taking form,
to see through the harsh lies which covered the ground she walked on.
All along she knew, and knowing was enough,
it gave her strength, it gave her courage above all else.
She protected me from all this,
when no one was protecting her.

Chantelle Lowe

Staying at places

I remember staying at people's places.
Moving around with my parents.
I remember sleeping in a very high,
soft bed.
So cosy and warm,
I felt safe.
While my parents were
working hard to free
someone.

Chantelle Lowe

Time ceases

This is the moment where time ceases,
and all around me I see what was.
I am gathered here to remember,
that all my suffering was not in vain.
I am surrounded by people who know,
and I know they made it.
Here I am,
amongst the feeling of strength.
This is my journey.

Chantelle Lowe

Photograph 10: Uluru at sunset, 17 August 1980.

Time on this world

A small envelope of time,
was all she had.
Does it really matter how much,
when that time was special?
Does it matter,
when she knew what it was to be loved?
A small amount of time,
and yet so significant.
A small hand, a small smile,
she touched others,
and I guess that is what really matters.

The witness (my mother)

She was a beautiful texture of purity on a road of cruelty,
the guiding light and fire which stood strong above lies and abuse.
Travelling forward a figure so elegant, tall and strong.
Wading through the darkest hours untouched,
sandy gold tresses flowing from her shoulders with confidence and sincerity.
Guiding the passages of time, one into another.
Real beauty, her beauty, comes from inside.
It envelopes her soul in a grace so rare, it remains unparalleled.
Her touch, so soft yet strong, with the vibrance of power in her voice.
Amidst all the harshness and cruelty she shone so bright,
It gave warmth and courage to others.
For this is the way it had to be, as others crumbled around her,
and she was offered no protection.
The elegant lady stood strong, holding her head high above the dirt,
as people tried to break her and slowly wear her down.
She had faith in herself, more than anyone could have thought.

She knew that she was too important to relent to those who sank in the mud.
Her confidence held her high as her innocent beliefs in justice shattered around her,
this was the worst thing she could ever face amidst the turmoil.
Time and time again she was called on to be stronger than those around her,
she knew that it was so important to continue on.
This woman, so elegant, so graceful, strove to see justice done,
it was faith, guiding her like a light in the rising darkness.
Even when hope had been lost her strength kept her from falling.
So beautiful as she glides atop the accusations and false remarks,
so serene is she inside when facing the cruelty of others,
and through all this she remained herself.

Chantelle Lowe

This is the path I walk on

This is the path I walk alone into the dim dark night.
I cry, and I do not remember,
what it is that I said.
In this world of misinterpretation
comes forth magnitude
of all the pressure that was upon them.
Here I am, I cannot laugh,
I cannot snigger,
for I know what is true.
It destroyed my childhood fantasies,
and gave me a life unparalleled
to those around me.
It took away my unlearned laughter,
and replaced it with a hollow pain,
creating an emptiness.
What is this life that I had?
I do not understand.

Chantelle Lowe

Why was I given this?
Why was I shown that I could not
believe in those who are all and mighty?
Why was I given this sight?
A burden rested on my shoulders for eternity.
I can no longer look up to people
that I am supposed to trust.
I can no longer respect others
on position alone.
I hid from the world
living in a private fear.

Chantelle Lowe

Waiting

I remember waiting with the
witnesses in the courthouse.
I remember my parents leaving,
and having to wait.
I remember waiting so long
for them to return.
Everyone was so serious,
and I was too young to be that way.

Chantelle Lowe

Where to turn

Amidst all the pain,
I see a light so strong.
It takes me away,
it sees me for who I am.
It picks me out,
and takes me into a world of disbelief.
Why did I have to know,
amidst so much wrong?
I watched helpless, and I knew,
God I knew,
and I didn't know what to do.
I didn't know where to turn,
and this was my world.

Whispering

Whispering in my ear,
whisper to hear.
Whisper what was,
when I was there.
Whisper of a time,
whisper of a frame of mind.
Whisper that I am there,
with people in kind.
This is what I feel,
so strong in mind is this,
that I know,
it is a celebration of life.

Chantelle Lowe

Undeciding factor

To the undeciding factor,
who am I?
I am the evidence of what was.
I am the rumour of what if.
I am something which held so true.
I am one, yet I am also another.
This is where I am.

Chantelle Lowe

Your name

Azaria, I will never forget your name,
you have a place in my heart.
A place so sacred and deep,
where I will never be the same.

It is hard to know where to start,
in this giant world of deceit.
Your soul was so fragile,
it showed the dark side of justice,
and proved your mother's faith.

www.ingramcontent.com/pod-product-compliance
Lightning Source LLC
Chambersburg PA
CBHW061134010526
44107CB00068B/2934